Extraordinary Leadership

GEMS MASTERY SERIES

TIMELESS LEADERSHIP PRINCIPLES FOR TODAY'S LEADERS

Quotes Compiled & Edited

by

DeCarlo A. Eskridge

NU DAE Enterprise Publications

United States of America

ISBN-13: 978-1468168594
ISBN-10: 1468168592

Edited by DeCarlo A. Eskridge
Cover Design ©NU DAE Enterprises, LLC, 2012
DeCarloEskridge.com

Printed in the United States of America

To my
lovely wife
Amanda

Acknowledgments

Jesus (1), Isaac Newton (2), Dwight D. Eisenhower (3), Winston Churchill (4, 54), John F. Kennedy (5), Napoleon Hill (6), Bill Gates (7), Albert Einstein (8, 58), Alvin Toffler (9), Henry Ford (10), Mahatma Gandhi (11), Harold R. McAlindon (12), Victor Cousin (13), Martin Luther King, Jr. (14), Napoleon Bonaparte (15), John Quincy Adams (16), Aristotle (17), John Adams (18), General Douglas MacArthur (19), Henry Miller (20), Edmund Spenser (21), George Orwell (22), Giuseppe Garibaldi (23), Dalia Grybauskaite (24), Thomas Carlyle (25), John Buchan (26), Theodore Roosevelt (27, 50, 64), Walter Lippman (28), Herbert B. Swope (29), Kenneth Blanchard (30), Eudora Welty (31), Lao Tzu (32, 68, 99), George Patton (33), The Bible (34), Horace (35), Cornelius Nepos (36), Solon (37), Ovid (38), Sophocles (39), Chinese Proverb (40), H. M. Tomlinson (41), Elbert Hubbard (42), Richard Bach (43), Machiavelli (44), John Cage (45), Richard B. Sheridan (46), Leo Tolstoy (47), Eleanor Roosevelt (48, 57), Japanese Proverb (49), Zig Ziglar (51), Johann Wolfgang von Goethe (52, 82, 118), Voltaire (53), Swami Vivekananda (55), Mark Twain (56, 88), Erica Jong (59), Friedrich Nietzsche (60), Ralph Waldo Emerson (61, 125), Henry David Thoreau (62, 98), Mark Wager (63), Bishop Desmond Tutu (65), Lewis H. Lapham (66), Ray Kroc (67), Andrew Carnegie (69), General John J. Pershing (70), Marian Anderson (71), Eric Hoffer (72), Marilyn Grey (73), Colonel Dandridge M. Malone (74), Abraham Lincoln (75), Baltasar Gracián (76), Vincent T. Lombardi (77), Adlai Stevenson (78), Sandra Carey (79), Thomas A. Edison (80), Ralph Nader (81), Noah Porter (83), Woodrow Wilson (84), Publius Syrus (85), James Thomas (86), Harry S. Truman (87, 95),

Seneca (89), Latin Proverb (90), Polybius (91), Donald Trump (96), Frank Tyger (97), Margaret Thatcher (100), Paul Tillich (101), Ella Wheeler Wilcox (102), Talleyrand (103), William Makepeace Thackeray (104), Harold Geneen (105), Susan L. Taylor (106),   Juliette Gordon Low (107), Sonia Gandhi (108), Peter Ustinov (109), Hannibal (110), Emmeline Pankhurst (111) Mart Church Terrell (112), LaDonna Harris (113) Ronald Reagan (114), Queen Elizabeth II (115), Maya Angelou (116), Angelina Grimke (117) William H. Johnson (119), George Herman "Babe" Ruth (120), Ross Perot (121), John C. Maxwell (122), Jack Welch (123), Colin Powell (124)

Introduction

If you could meet any one person in history and ask that person one question; who would you pick and what would you ask? The Gem Mastery Series of books is a compilation of quotes from some of the greatest leaders, innovators, and business people of all time. These powerful, little books are for anyone seeking motivation and inspiration to achieve their dreams - whether it is to become a better person, a more successful business person, a more effective leader or whatever your dream - you have the ability to facilitate the change you desire. You are about to discover some wonderful inspirational quotes that will leap out from the page providing you with exactly what you need, when you need it. These gems of wisdom will supply you with the energy and motivation necessary to take action and achieve all that you are capable of achieving.

In this book, you will discover timeless gems (*quotes*) from some of the world's most influential leaders. Leaders and innovators, who have turned their values into action and, in the process, changed the way the world does business. This book is required reading for all who are in positions of leadership and/or those who support those in leadership positions. In order to get the most from your reading, we recommend that you read **Extraordinary Leadership** until you master the precious gems within.

Whoever desires to become great must learn to serve.

- Jesus

Of I have seen farther than others, it is because I was standing on the shoulder of giants.

- Isaac Newton

♦

$\mathcal{L}$eadership: the art of getting someone else to do something you want done because he wants to do it.

- Dwight D. Eisenhower

♦

The price of greatness is responsibility.

- **Winston Churchill**

◆

$\mathcal{L}$eadership and learning are indispensable to each other.

- John F. Kennedy

♦

$\mathcal{D}$esire is the starting
point of all achievement,
not a hope, not a wish, but
a keen pulsating desire
which transcends
everything.

- Napoleon Hill

♦

$\mathcal{A}$s we look ahead into the next century, leaders will be those who empower others.

- Bill Gates

The significant problems
we face cannot be solved
at the same level of
thinking we were at when
we created them.

- Albert Einstein

♦

You've got to think
about big things while
you're doing small things,
so that all the small things
go in the right direction.

- Alvin Toffler

◆

$\mathcal{I}$f you think you can do
a thing or that you cannot
do a thing, in either case
you are right.

- Henry Ford

♦

$\mathcal{Y}$ou must be the change you want to see in the world.

- Mahatma Gandhi

Do not follow where the
path may lead.
Go instead where there is
no path and leave a trail.

- Harold R. McAlindon

♦

$\mathcal{M}$en are governed only by serving them; the rule is without exception.

- Victor Cousin

$\mathcal{T}$he ultimate measure of a man is not where he stands in moments of comfort, but where he stands at times of challenge and controversy.

- Martin Luther King, Jr.

♦

$\mathcal{A}$ leader is a dealer in hope.

- Napoleon Bonaparte

◆

$\mathscr{O}$f your actions inspire others to dream more, learn more, do more and become more, you are a leader.

- John Quincy Adams

♦

*H*e who has never
learned to obey
cannot be a good
commander.

- Aristotle

♦

Of we do not lay out ourselves in the service of mankind whom should we serve?

- John Adams

◆

$\mathcal{A}$ general is just as good or just as bad as the troops under his command make him.

- General Douglas MacArthur

◆

The real leader has no
need to lead --
he is content to point the
way.

- Henry Miller

♦

All can he rule the great
that cannot reach the small.

- Edmund Spenser

◆

*H*igh sentiments always win in the end, The leaders who offer blood, toil, tears and sweat always get more out of their followers than those who offer safety and a good time. When it comes to the pinch, human beings are heroic.

- George Orwell

♦

$\mathcal{A}$ bold onset is half the battle.

- Giuseppe Garibaldi

Crisis is an opportunity. It cannot be avoided so take advantage of it. We must seize this unique opportunity to reshape the world to meet the challenges of the 21st century.

- Dalia Grybauskaite

◆

$\mathcal{L}$et him who would be moved to convince others, be first moved to convince himself.

- Thomas Carlyle

♦

The task of leadership is not to put greatness into people, but to elicit it, for the greatness is there already.

- John Buchan

◆

The best executive is the one who has sense enough to pick good men to do what he wants done, and self-restraint to keep from meddling with them while they do it.

- Theodore Roosevelt

♦

The final test of a leader
is that he leaves behind
him in other men, the
conviction and the will to
carry on.

- Walter Lippman

♦

$\mathcal{I}$ cannot give you the formula for success, but I can give you the formula for failure: which is: Try to please everybody.

- Herbert B. Swope

♦

The key to successful
leadership today
is influence,
not authority.

- Kenneth Blanchard

♦

All serious daring starts from within.

- Eudora Welty

$\mathcal{G}$o to the people. Learn from them. Live with them. Start with what they know. Build with what they have. The best of leaders when the job is done, when the task is accomplished, the people will say we have done it ourselves.

- Lao Tzu

♦

*N*ever tell people how to do things. Tell them what to do and they will surprise you with their ingenuity.

- General George Patton

◆

$\mathcal{W}$here there is no
vision, the people perish.

- The Bible

♦

$\mathcal{M}$isfortunes, untoward events, lay open, disclose the skill of a general, while success conceals his weakness, his weak points.

- Horace

♦

The power is detested, and miserable the life, of him who wishes to be feared rather than to be loved.

- Cornelius Nepos

◆

$\mathcal{H}$e who has learned how to obey will know how to command.

- Solon

$\mathcal{A}$ ruler should be slow to punish and swift to reward.

- Ovid

What you cannot
enforce /
do not command.

- Sophocles

♦

The man who removes a mountain begins by carrying away small stones.

- Chinese Proverb

◆

We see things not as they are, but as we are.

- H. M. Tomlinson

$\mathcal{T}$o avoid criticism do nothing, say nothing, be nothing.

- **Elbert Hubbard**

◆

Sooner or later, those who win are those who think they can.

- Richard Bach

$\mathcal{W}$here the willingness is
great, the difficulties
cannot be great.

- Machiavelli

♦

$\mathcal{I}$can't understand why people are frightened by new ideas. I'm frightened by old ones.

- John Cage

◆

The surest way not to fail
is to determine to succeed.

- **Richard B. Sheridan**

♦

Everyone thinks of changing the world, but no one thinks of changing himself.

- Leo Tolstoy

♦

Great minds discuss
ideas;
Average minds discuss
events;
Small minds discuss
people.

- Eleanor Roosevelt

◆

*V*ision without action is
daydream. Action without
vision is nightmare.

- Japanese Proverb

In any situation, the best thing you can do is the right thing; the next best thing you can do is the wrong thing; the worst thing you can do is nothing.

- Theodore Roosevelt

◆

$\mathcal{Y}$ou can get everything in life you want if you will just help enough other people get what they want.

- Zig Ziglar

◆

What you get by achieving your goals is not as important as what you become by achieving your goals.

- Johann Wolfgang von Goethe

◆

$\mathcal{A}$ppreciation is a wonderful thing: It makes what is excellent in others belong to us as well.

- **Voltaire**

♦

$\mathcal{I}$f you're going through
hell, keep going.

- Winston Churchill

◆

$\mathcal{T}$ake up one idea. Make that one idea your life – think of it, dream of it, and live on idea. Let the brain, muscles, nerves, every part of your body, be full of that idea, and just leave every other idea alone. This is the way to success.

- **Swami Vivekananda**

*K*eep away from people who try to belittle your ambitions. Small people always do that, but the really great make you feel that you, too, can become great.

- **Mark Twain**

♦

It is not fair to ask of others what you are not willing to do yourself.

- Eleanor Roosevelt

♦

$\mathcal{T}$ry not to become a man of success but a man of value.

- Albert Einstein

♦

The trouble is, if you don't risk anything, you risk even more.

- Erica Jong

♦

$\mathcal{H}$e who has a why to live can bear almost any how.

- Friedrich Nietzsche

◆

What lies behind us and what lies before us are tiny matters compared to what lies within us.

- Ralph Waldo Emerson

$\mathcal{D}$o not worry if you have built your castles in the air. They are where they should be. Now put the foundations under them.

- Henry David Thoreau

♦

The greatest lesson of leadership is learning that it's never about you.

- Mark Wager

♦

People ask the difference between a leader and a boss. The leader works in the open, and the boss in covert. The leader leads, and the boss drives.

- Theodore Roosevelt

◆

$\mathcal{I}$ am a leader by default, only because nature does not allow a vacuum.

- Bishop Desmond Tutu

$\mathcal{L}$eadership consists not in degrees of technique but in traits of character; it requires moral rather than athletic or intellectual effort, and it imposes on both leader and follower alike the burdens of self-restraint.

- Lewis H. Lapham

♦

The quality of a leader is reflected in the standards they set for themselves.

- Ray Kroc

♦

When the effective
leader is finished with his
work, the people say that it
happened naturally.

- Lao Tzu

♦

$\mathcal{N}$o man will make a great leader who wants to do it all himself, or to get all the credit for doing it.

- Andrew Carnegie

◆

A competent leader can get efficient service from poor troops, while on the contrary an incapable leader can demoralize the best of troops.

- General John J. Pershing

♦

$\mathcal{L}$eadership should be
born out of the
understanding of the needs
of those who would be
affected by it.

- Marian Anderson

◆

The leader has to be practical and a realist, yet must talk the language of the visionary and the idealist.

- Eric Hoffer

◆

We know not where our dreams will take us, but we can probably see quite clearly where we'll go without them.

- Marilyn Grey

♦

$\mathcal{T}$he very essence of leadership is its purpose. And the purpose of leadership is to accomplish a task. That is what leadership does--and what it does is more important than what it is or how it works.

- Colonel Dandridge M. Malone

*N*early all men can stand adversity, but if you want to test a man's character, give him power.

- Abraham Lincoln

♦

$\mathscr{Be}$ known for pleasing others, especially if you govern them… Ruling other has one advantage: you can do more good than anyone else.

- **Baltasar Gracián**

♦

The quality of a person's life is in direct proportion to their commitment to excellence, regardless of their chosen field of endeavor.

- Vincent T. Lombardi

♦

*U*nderstanding human
needs is half the job of
meeting them.

- Adlai Stevenson

◆

$\mathcal{N}$ever mistake knowledge for wisdom. One helps you make a living; the other helps you make a life.

- Sandra Carey

◆

*H*ell, there are no rules here — we're trying to accomplish something.

- Thomas A. Edison

♦

$\mathcal{I}$start with the premise that the function of leadership is to produce more leaders, not more followers.

- Ralph Nader

♦

$\mathcal{W}$hat chance gathers
she easily scatters. A great
person attracts great people
and knows how to hold
them together.

- **Johann Wolfgang von Goethe**

◆

ℛely on your own strength of body and soul. Take for your star self-reliance, faith, honesty and industry. Don't take too much advice — keep at the helm and steer your own ship, and remember that the great art of commanding is to take a fair share of the work. Fire above the mark you intend to hit. Energy, invincible determination with the right motive, are the levers that move the world.

- Noah Porter

♦

*L*eadership does not always wear the harness of compromise.

- **Woodrow Wilson**

♦

The greater a man is in power above others, the more he ought to excel them in virtue. None ought to govern who is not better than the governed.

- Publius Syrus

◆

$\mathcal{T}$o be a great leader and so always master of the situation, one must of necessity have been a great thinker in action.

- James Thomas

♦

$\mathcal{I}$ never did give anybody hell, I just told the truth, and they thought it was hell.

- Harry S. Truman

♦

Success is a journey, not a destination. It requires constant effort, vigilance and re-evaluation.

- Mark Twain

◆

It is impossible to imagine anything which better becomes a ruler than mercy.

- Seneca

It is absurd that a man should rule others, who cannot rule himself.

- Latin Proverb

♦

$\mathcal{A}$ good general not only sees the way to victory; he also knows when victory is impossible.

- Polybius

♦

The very essence of leadership is that you have to have vision. You can't blow an uncertain trumpet.

- Theodore M. Hesburgh

♦

$\mathcal{I}$ think leadership comes from integrity – that you do whatever you ask others to do. I think there are non-obvious ways to lead. Just by providing a good example as a parent, a friend, a neighbor makes it possible for other people to see better ways to do things. Leadership does not need to be a dramatic, fist in the air and trumpets blaring, activity.

- **Scott Berkun**

♦

The leaders who work most effectively, it seems to me, never say "I." And that's not because they have trained themselves not to say "I." They don't think "I." They think "we"; they think "team." They understand their job to be to make the team function. They accept responsibility and don't sidestep it, but "we" gets the credit…. This is what creates trust, what enables you to get the task done.

- Peter Drucker

$\mathcal{M}$en make history and
not the other way around.
In periods where there is
no leadership, society
stands still. Progress
occurs when courageous,
skillful leaders seize the
opportunity to change
things for the better.

- Harry Truman

♦

$\mathcal{A}$s long as you are going
to be thinking anyway,
THINK BIG!

- Donald Trump

♦

Your future depends on many things, but mostly on you.

- Frank Tyger

♦

If one advances confidently in the direction of his dreams, and endeavors to live the life which he has imagined, he will meet with success unexpected in common hours.

- Henry David Thoreau

♦

He who controls others may be powerful, but he who has mastered himself is mightier still.

- Lao Tzu

◆

$\mathcal{D}$isciplining yourself to do what you know is right and importance, although difficult, is the high road to pride, self-esteem, and personal satisfaction.

- Margaret Thatcher

♦

$\mathcal{M}$an is asked to make of himself what he is supposed to become to fulfill his destiny.

- Paul Tillich

◆

There is no chance, no destiny, no fate, that can circumvent or hinder or control the firm resolve of a determined soul.

- Ella Wheeler Wilcox

♦

$\mathscr{I}$am more afraid of an army of 100 sheep led by a lion than an army of 100 lions led by a sheep.

- **Talleyrand**

♦

$\mathcal{N}$ever lose a chance of saying a kind word.

- William Makepeace Thackeray

♦

$\mathcal{A}$ true leader has to have a genuine open-door policy so that his people are not afraid to approach him for any reason.

- Harold Geneen

♦

In every crisis there is a message. Crises are nature's way of forcing change – breaking down old structures, shaking loose negative habits so that something new and better can take their place.

- Susan L. Taylor

♦

The work of today is the history of tomorrow, and we are its makers.

- Juliette Gordon Low

♦

Power in itself has never attracted me, nor has position been my goal. My resolve will in fact be all the more firm, to fight for our principles, for our vision, and for our ideals.

- Sonia Gandhi

♦

$\mathcal{A}$t the age of four with paper hats and wooden swords we're all Generals. Only some of us never grow out of it.

- Peter Ustinov

♦

He will either find a
way, or make one.

- Hannibal

*T*hose men and women are fortunate who are born at a time when great struggle for human freedom is in progress.

- Emmeline Pankhurst

♦

$\mathcal{L}$ifting as they climb, onward and upward they go, struggling and striving and hoping that the buds and blossoms of their desires may burst into glorious fruition ere long.

\- Mart Church Terrell

$\mathcal{L}$eadership is a communal responsibility with a concern for the welfare of the people or tribe and then sharing the work that needs to be done based on skills and abilities. Leadership is shared responsibility and promoting people's well-being.

- LaDonna Harris

♦

$\mathcal{T}$o grasp and hold a vision, that is the very essence of successful leadership – not only in the movie set where I learnt it, but everywhere.

- Ronald Reagan

◆

$\mathcal{I}$cannot lead you into battle. I do not give you laws or administer justice, but I can do something else – I can give my heart and my devotion to these old islands and to all the peoples of our brotherhood of nations.

- Queen Elizabeth II

$\mathcal{I}$'ve learned that people will forget what you said, people will forget what you did, but people will never forget how you made them feel.

- Maya Angelou

♦

Of a law commands me
to sin I will break it;
if it calls me to suffer,
I will let it take its course
unresistingly. The doctrine
of the blind obedience and
unqualified submission to
any human power, whether
civil or ecclesiastical, is
the doctrine of despotism,
and ought to have no place.

- Angelina Grimke

♦

Things which matter most must never be at the mercy of things which matter least.

- Johann Wolfgang von Goethe

◆

Of it is to be,
it is up to me.

- William H. Johnson

I hit big or I miss big.
I like to live as big as I am.

- George Herman "Babe" Ruth

◆

*L*ead and inspire people. Don't try to manage and manipulate people. Inventories can be managed but people must be lead.

- Ross Perot

♦

$\mathcal{A}$ leader is one who knows the way, goes the way, and shows the way.

- John C. Maxwell

♦

$\mathscr{B}$efore you are a leader,
success is all about
growing yourself. When
you become a leader,
success is all about
growing others.

- Jack Welch

◆

$\mathcal{L}$eadership is solving problems. The day soldiers stop bringing you their problems is the day you have stopped leading them. They have either lost confidence that you can help or concluded you do not care. Either case is a failure of leadership.

- Colin Powell

♦

$\mathcal{O}$ur chief want is someone who will inspire us to be what we know we could be.

- Ralph Waldo Emerson

♦

About the Author

DeCarlo A. Eskridge is a spiritual life-coach/ trainer, host of Blogtalk Radio's "Live Your Greatness," motivational speaker, certified hypnotherapist, certified N.L.P. practitioner/ trainer, author, and minister. He is very proud to have authored and independently-published several books through his company NU DAE Enterprises where he serves as President and CEO.

A prolific teacher and encourager, DeCarlo A. Eskridge reads over 50 books a year, and listens to countless hours of audio programs. He is a Certified Life Coach through Franklin Covey and a motivational speaker who earned advanced honors at Toastmasters International. He is also an Ordained Minister with over 25 years of biblical study.

DeCarlo A. Eskridge has been imbued with an inexhaustible, unyielding, and unrelenting thirst and hunger for knowledge. His mission is to travel the globe teaching, empowering, inspiring, and transforming the lives of millions with the truths he has discovered in order that every person recognizes who he or she is, what he or she can accomplish, and that they live it!

GEMS MASTERY SERIES

NU DAE Enterprise Publications

DeCarloEskridge.com

ISBN-13: 978-1468168594
ISBN-10: 1468168592